# Everglades
# Country

# Everglades Country
## A QUESTION OF
## LIFE OR DEATH

**Patricia Lauber**

Photographs by
Patricia Caufield

THE VIKING PRESS   NEW YORK

Cover photo: *A great white heron, a*
*fish eater, watches and waits for prey in*
*the shallow water near red mangrove prop roots.*

Pages 8–9: *A bald eagle lands on the tree where its nest is.*

*First Edition*

Text copyright © 1973 by Patricia Lauber
Photographs copyright © 1973 by Patricia Caulfield
All rights reserved
First published in 1973 by The Viking Press, Inc.
625 Madison Avenue, New York, N.Y. 10022
Published simultaneously in Canada by
The Macmillan Company of Canada Limited
Library of Congress catalog card number: 72–9909

PRINTED IN U.S.A.     1   2   3   4   5   77   76   75   74   73

574.5  Ecology      SBN 670–30022–5

*Acknowledgments*

The author is indebted to the many persons concerned about the future of Everglades National Park who assisted her with her research by giving generously of their time and special knowledge and by directing her to special publications. In particular, she would like to thank the following persons:

At the University of Miami, *Dr. Durbin Tabb* of the Rosenstiel School of Marine and Atmospheric Science and *Arthur R. Marshall* of The Center for Urban Studies.

At United States Geological Survey, Miami, *Dr. Milton C. Kolipinski, James W. Hartwell,* and *Aaron Higer.*

At Everglades National Park, *Dr. William B. Robertson, Jr.,* chief park naturalist; *John Ogden III* and *Richard Klukas,* biologists; *Francis Nix,* hydrologist; *Erwin Winte,* district ranger; *Ralph Miele,* park pilot; and *Dale Engquist* and *Betty Poff* of the administrative staff.

# CONTENTS

# Everglades Country

# Turning Point

In early autumn of 1968 work began on a new jetport in south Florida. Bulldozers moved into a swamp called Big Cypress, uprooting trees and leveling land as the first step in clearing, draining, and filling the site.

The long-range plans called for a gigantic installation, covering thirty-nine square miles. Five times the size of Kennedy International Airport in New York, the jetport was to be the biggest and most modern of its kind. Take-offs and landings were expected to occur every thirty seconds. Two six-mile-long runways would handle supersonic jets. Passenger terminals, control towers, hangars, air freight facilities sprouted in clusters on the plans. In addition, there was to be a thousand-foot-wide transportation corridor, containing an interstate highway and a high-speed rail system to link Miami on the east coast with Naples on the west. The planners foresaw the growth of aerospace industries near the jetport. And because of the number of people who would work at the

*American and snowy egrets usually*
*rest in groups at night, then take*
*off in soaring flight at dawn to feed.*

jetport and in the industries, a whole city would spring up. By 1980, it was believed, one and a half million people would be living and working in what was now just a piece of swamp.

The planners saw no real problems ahead, no obstacles that men and machines could not overcome. The jetport would be acclaimed as another triumph of man over nature.

But that was not the case. When the plans became known, a storm of criticism arose. As the storm gathered force, work on the jetport was brought to a halt. And in 1970 the federal, state, and county governments agreed to end the project. A new jetport was needed to relieve Miami's crowded, busy airport. But it would have to be built somewhere else, not in this corner of Big Cypress Swamp.

The halting of the jetport marked a turning point in the history of Florida and perhaps of the United States, for in this land of plenty people had always believed that growth was good and bigger was better. For fifty years developers had been carving up south Florida, draining, filling, clearing, building, and paving it over. The population boomed, and so did land values and business.

Few persons ever looked beyond the most immediate consequences of what was being done. Few ever wondered what else might happen if . . . if the coastal mangrove swamps were leveled and filled in to make land for houses . . . if the inland marshes were cleared and drained to open them up for farming and towns. The few

Men armed with machines like this
giant bulldozer had started leveling
part of Big Cypress Swamp to make a jetport, when the project was brought to a halt.

persons who did worry about how the land was being changed were lonely voices, often accused of interfering with progress or of thinking that birds were more important than people.

Then in the late 1960s a great many people suddenly started to worry about the environment, about what man and modern technology were doing to it. "Ecology"— the science that deals with the relationship of living things to their environment—became an everyday word. It was this concern with ecology that halted the jetport. For perhaps the first time, many people really understood that the true cost of a giant project cannot be measured in dollars alone. Cost must also be measured in terms of the environment. That understanding was the turning point.

The thirty-nine square miles could be carved out of Big Cypress Swamp and cleared. The jetport could be built, along with the highway, rail system, factories, and houses. It would cost hundreds of millions of dollars, but it would, the planners said, pay for itself, besides creating jobs, industries, and a whole city.

Scientists, however, were looking beyond these immediate results. They were looking at what else the jetport would do in south Florida. And they foresaw disaster. The jetport would destroy the ecosystem, the web of life, in south Florida by producing four million gallons of sewage each day and ten thousand tons of jet engine pollutants each year. That was the finding of a long careful study prepared by the United States Department of the Interior. Among the victims would be Everglades National Park, which lay only six miles south of the proposed jetport and received part of its water from Big Cypress in a slow overland flow.

Everglades is unique among national parks, for it was created as a park of life, of plants and animals. All are tied to their environment, to a watery land of marshes and swamps. Water is life to the park, water that creeps in a thin film over the land for months at a time. Of the water that supports the park, one third comes from Big Cypress, and it is the only water that flows freely and naturally into the park. Without that flow of pure fresh water, the park would be at best greatly changed and at worst doomed.

The realization that the true price of the jetport included the destruction of a national park halted the project. The price was too high, and so work was stopped in Big Cypress and the park was saved.

Or was it? That was the question facing many concerned scientists and conservationists.

The park had certainly been saved from the pollution of the jetport. But other serious threats were looming, and the park was already staggering under burdens created by years of short-sighted development in south Florida. Ecological studies are continuing, and they raise grave questions about the future of this treasure house of life.

# A Park of Life    2

Early summer's noonday sun blazes out of a cloudless blue sky, its heat stilling the park. Almost everywhere the animal world has taken refuge, in trees and holes and burrows, under leaves and stones, wherever there is shade or coolness to be found. Only in the water is there movement, and it is slow.

In Taylor Slough,* which resembles a large clear pond, fish are swimming. A large-mouthed bass lazily pursues a little sunfish. Big cigar-shaped garfish wiggle past. A large turtle waddles across the bottom. A water-logged tree trunk comes to life and begins to swim. It is not a piece of tree after all, but an alligator. Propelled by its powerful tail, the alligator glides through the water, with only the top of its back and head showing above the surface. An anhinga, sometimes called the snakebird or water turkey, perches motionless on a tree branch over-

---

* Rhymes with *flew.* A slough is a low-lying wet area that is longer than it is wide.

*The magnificent frigate, or man-of-war, bird summers around the Florida Keys, flying south to breed on Caribbean islands in the winter. Soaring with an unmatched ease, the frigate bird steals many of its meals by harassing other fish feeders until they drop their catch, which the frigate captures in mid-air.*

looking the slough, its head turned to the side and its four-foot-wide wings spread in the sun. Even in the most quiet hours of the most quiet season there is always something for the patient watcher to see in Everglades National Park.

Tucked in the southern tip of Florida, Everglades is the third largest national park. It is nearly twice the size of Rhode Island, containing some one and a half million acres of land and water. Everglades is, like the other parks, a piece of wilderness set aside to be preserved in its natural state. But in one way it stands alone. Other parks were established to preserve geological or scenic features of the North American continent. Everglades was established to protect and preserve the many forms of life within its boundaries. Here are no soaring snow-capped mountains, no geysers, no giant canyons, no glaciers. This is a park of life: of birds and mammals, of fish, reptiles, and amphibians, and of plants.

For this reason, strange as it may seem, a new visitor is likely to feel disappointed. The big park is flat and open, and during part of the year much of it lies under a foot or two of water. At first glance it is a vast expanse of scrubby plants dotted here and there with humped islands of trees. The visitor's eye, used to more spectacular scenery, in the beginning sees nothing. The park's quiet charm grows upon acquaintance, for Everglades yields its treasures slowly. The interesting plants must be sought out. Wildlife is where you find it. What you find and where you find it varies both with the season and the hour of day.

During the course of a year, more than three hundred species of birds can be seen in the park. Some are native to south Florida, while others are migrants, flying north or south with the seasons and perhaps wintering in the park.

There are many familiar land birds — towhees, cardinals, blue jays, bobwhites, meadowlarks, red-winged blackbirds. Wild turkeys may be seen around live oaks, where they find and eat acorns. Sometimes a pileated woodpecker can be heard chopping a hole in a tree trunk.

Birds of prey are numerous. There is the night hunter, the owl, swooping down to catch a mouse, rabbit, snail, or insect. There are vultures, whose circling flight signals a death on the ground. Hawks hunt small mammals, frogs, and lizards. About thirty pairs of bald eagles nest in the park, most of them on mangrove islands in Florida Bay. In south Florida these big, rare birds eat mostly fish. They often pick up dead fish from the shore, but they are also expert fishermen, having sharp sight, strong claws, and a sturdy hooked beak.

The familiar shore birds are all to be found — terns and gulls fishing the coastal waters, long-legged sandpipers and plovers stalking their food on the tidal mud flats, ducks and coots floating on the waters of marshes and lakes.

A less common shore bird is the black skimmer, which is known by a number of names: the sea dog (for its loud barklike cry), the scissorbill (for its four-inch-long scissor-like bill), and the cutwater (for the way that it slices the water with its bill). When feeding, the skimmer flies low over the water with its bill open. The lower part cuts through the water. When it strikes a shrimp or a small fish, the bill quickly closes and the skimmer snatches its catch from the water.

Another shore bird, the purple gallinule, is so unlikely a creature that it hardly seems real. About the size of a large chicken, this marsh dweller has glossy blue, green, and purple feathers, a red beak with a yellow tip, long bright yellow legs, and big webless feet. Sometimes it appears to be walking on water. (It is actually walking on lily pads and feeding on the insects, snails, and other creatures that it finds among them.) The gallinule swims well, but it looks awkward in flight because its long legs dangle beneath its body. On land the gallinule climbs bushes and trees in order to perch in them. Time and patience (or luck) are needed to see a purple gallinule walking on water. But the park has many big water birds that are easy to see and that are the star attractions.

One of these is the anhinga, which is seen around tree-fringed fresh-water ponds and sloughs. The anhinga is sometimes called the water turkey, perhaps because of its glossy dark plumage. It is also known as the snake-bird because only its small head and long slender neck show above the water when it swims, and it looks very much like a swimming snake. The anhinga is a spear fisherman, armed with a long sharp bill. It stalks its prey underwater, spears the fish with a quick thrust of its bill, and then carries its catch to shore. The fish is tossed in the air, caught, and swallowed. When the anhinga has

*Cypress grows in low-lying areas that are flooded part of the year. What look like tree stumps in this photograph are actually cypress knees, growths thought to serve as breathing organs for the trees when the land is under water.*

finished fishing, it retreats to a perch and spreads its wings to dry. The feathers are wet because the anhinga lacks the oil glands of other water birds, which coat feathers and keep them from becoming water-soaked.

Among the many wading birds, the roseate spoonbill is the most eye-catching. An adult spoonbill has bright pink feathers, long red legs, red eyes, and a long bill with a flat, spoon-shaped tip. It feeds by wading in shallow water and swinging its bill back and forth in the mud. Bottom debris swirls into the bill and is tested against the many nerve endings inside the wide spoon. Minnows, shrimp, insects, and other living organisms are swallowed. Mud and other inorganic matter is washed out. One of the great treats in the park is to walk along a quiet path near the shore and suddenly glimpse through a tangle of mangroves a pair of spoonbills feeding in a pond or inlet. Nearby a big white ibis may be probing the mud with its long slim bill, searching for snails, crayfish, or shrimp.

Various kinds of herons can be seen in the park, among them the great white heron and the great blue, which are two of the largest wading birds in North America. Stately and slow-moving, they are often seen standing motionless in shallow salty water, poised to strike at shrimp, fish, and other prey. Among the herons are the birds called egrets. One, the reddish egret, is now very rare but can be immediately recognized by anyone lucky enough to see it fishing. Unlike other wading birds, which stalk their prey slowly and silently, the reddish egret runs, stumbles, lurches, and dashes about the shallows and mud flats. Frightened fish seek safety in the shadows of the egret's outspread wings—and are seized and eaten.

The brown pelican is also impossible to mistake, for it has a huge wingspan of six and a half feet and a long, flat, pouched bill. Brown pelicans are common in areas where fishing boats come in and handouts are plentiful, and they can be seen feeding near the docks or resting atop pilings, with heads and necks hunched into the shoulders. They are, however, excellent fishermen themselves. A brown pelican flies over the shallow water until it sees a suitable fish. Then it executes a power dive, plunging into the water with a noisy splash and scooping up the fish in its pouch.

White pelicans are migrants from the north that winter in the park. Like the browns, they have large pouches, but they seldom dive for fish. Instead, a white pelican swims or wades, using its pouch as a net to dip fish out of the water.

The pelicans have an interesting relative, the frigate bird, also called the man-of-war bird, which is a summer visitor from the south. It has extremely short legs, so short that the frigate bird is nearly helpless on the ground. But it is one of the most agile acrobats of the air. It can turn, dive, hang in the wind, or put on a burst of speed. A frigate bird may pick up a fish swimming near the surface or snatch a flying fish out of the air. But it is even more likely to rob gulls, pelicans, or other sea birds of their catch. The frigate bird harasses the other bird until the victim disgorges the fish. Then the frigate bird neatly catches the prize in mid-air.

The frigate bird is rivaled in agility only by the swallow-tailed kite, another visitor from the south. The kite, which is a hawk and a bird of prey, has long narrow wings and a deeply forked tail. It is so agile that it catches its food in flight, may eat in flight, and can swoop to drink without landing. The swallow-tailed kite eats large insects, frogs, lizards, small snakes, and nestling birds, lifting its prey out of treetops in the course of graceful soaring flight.

Given the richness and variety of its bird life, the park seems rather poor in mammals, of which it has only about thirty species. The reason for this great difference is that birds can fly. They can readily cross land barriers, such as mountains and swamps. They can cross open water. Mammals cross land barriers only with difficulty. Land mammals seldom cross a sea barrier without the help of man. That is why relatively few mammals have reached the southern tip of Florida.

Florida is a peninsula that reaches southward, like a paw, from the body of North America. Compared with the rest of the continent, the peninsula is new land; it has been above water for only a few thousand years. Its animals and plants are ones that have spread into Florida from other regions. Birds, traveling by air, have come from both north and south. Mammals, traveling mostly by land, have come chiefly from the north. Except for one or two kinds of bats (air travelers from the south), they are all mammals known in eastern North America: cottontails and marsh rabbits, flying squirrels, gray squirrels, and fox squirrels, various kinds of rats and mice, shrews, skunks, mink, otters, wildcats, panthers, black bears, gray foxes, white-tailed deer, raccoons, and opossums.

The panthers and bears are rare and seldom seen. The wildcat, however, which looks like an overgrown house-cat with a short tail, is often seen in early morning or early evening. Deer are numerous and can be seen around

*Wading birds, such as egrets and wood storks, share this brackish backwater with ducks and white pelicans.*

dawn or twilight, when they are out feeding. Raccoons
are everywhere, robbing garbage cans, fishing, catching
fiddler crabs, climbing a tree for its fruit, stealing eggs
from nests. Otters are seen in many of the fresh-water
areas, where they feed mostly on fish, snakes, frogs,
turtles, and sometimes on baby alligators. With their
sleek streamlined bodies and short legs, otters are more
at home in the water than on land and are strong, graceful swimmers.

The park's coastal waters and tidal rivers hold two
kinds of water-dwelling mammals, the manatee and the
bottle-nosed dolphin. The manatee is a strange-looking
creature with a large plump body, perhaps thirteen feet
long and weighing half a ton, that is sparsely covered
with bristly hairs. It has paddle-like flippers and a flat-
tened tail. The manatee swims by sweeping its broad tail
up and down. It feeds on pastures of grasslike marine
plants that grow in shallow bays and lagoons. The bottle-
nose is a member of the whale family, a fish eater, and
an animal that is often seen because it swims beside boats
and leaps and plays around them.

Like the mammals, most of the reptiles and amphibians
in south Florida belong to species that came from the
north. The only exceptions are the crocodiles, which,
like a few species of frogs and lizards, reached south
Florida from the West Indies. And so the park does not
offer the same great variety of these animals that it does
of birds. In addition, many of these animals live quietly
hidden away and are seldom seen by human visitors.

The three or four kinds of salamander, for example, are

almost invisible, because these amphibians live beneath the thick plant cover of ponds and canals. The frogs, which include tiny tree frogs and big bullfrogs, are sometimes seen, but their vast number becomes apparent only when the summer rains and breeding season begin. Then each night brings a tremendous chorus of frog voices.

The reptiles of the park include lizards, turtles, snakes, alligators, and crocodiles. Of these the alligator is the easiest to see, and it is the reptile that park visitors find most fascinating. This long dark creature is a relic of a vanished age — the age of dinosaurs. Alligators and dinosaurs were descended from the same distant relative, and there were alligators in the days of dinosaurs. The dinosaurs died out, but the alligators survived, a reminder of a world ruled by giant reptiles. The park's alligators live chiefly in fresh-water areas. At the times of year when water floods the park, they appear almost everywhere. When the park goes dry, they retreat to the deeper ponds and sloughs, where they float, swim, submerge, or clamber out to sun themselves.

More than a million people visit the park each year. They come for the alligators and the spoonbills, for the plant life, for fishing. They come for pleasure and recreation, for a sense of finding their roots, of getting back to nature. Here they can experience what much of south Florida was like before the coming of white men, for the park preserves a small part of a huge region that was unlike any other in North America: the Everglades. It preserves a small part of the great wilderness, the river of grass, that once filled the center of south Florida.

# A River of Grass    3

The Everglades was a river. Like any other river, it had a channel through which water flowed from higher to lower ground as it moved toward the sea. It had a place where it began: Okeechobee, the large lake in the center of Florida. It had a place where it ended, where its waters met the sea: the tidal estuaries of the Gulf of Mexico and of Florida Bay. Here the resemblance to other rivers ended. The Everglades was not the kind of river that appears on maps as a thin blue line.

Sweeping in an arc through south Florida, the Everglades was only about one hundred twenty miles long, but it was, on the average, forty miles wide. Its waters were seldom more than two feet deep, and they flowed so slowly that they seemed to lie unmoving, like a lens upon the land.

Draining toward the sea, the water wove its way through vast tracts of saw grass, broken only by occasional islands of trees. Saw grass is the plant most char-

*Saw grass, the plant most character-istic of the Everglades, blooms with a brown flower and produces a brown seed.*

acteristic of the Everglades, and that is why the region has been called a "river of grass" and why the Indians named it *Pa-hay-okee*, meaning Grassy Water. Saw grass, however, is really a sedge, not a grass. A true grass has a round hollow stem, whereas a sedge has a triangular solid one, usually with sharp edges. The blades of saw grass are edged with tiny sawlike teeth, as sharp as points of glass.

In the northern Everglades the saw grass grew thick and tall, as tall as fifteen feet. Farther south its stands were less dense, and it grew to heights of four to six feet. Wherever it grew, saw grass was the plant that created the Everglades, that laid a covering of soil over the bare limestone that had risen from the sea. For hundreds and hundreds of years, saw grass sprang up out of the shallow river, lived, and died. The dead saw grass decayed and, in rotting, began to lay down a thick layer of peat.

The peat covered the limestone. Like a sponge, it absorbed water, stored it, and then released it to go its way. In time, the vast river of grass took shape, curving south from Okeechobee and covering twenty-eight hundred square miles of central Florida.

The river was seasonal, depending on the rains for water. Then, as now, the rains fell only at certain times of year.

The climate of south Florida is like that of a tropical island, for the land reaches close to the tropics and is nearly surrounded by water. It is washed by warm sea waters on three sides and is bordered on the north by the seven hundred square miles of shallow water in Lake Okeechobee. As in the tropics, there are two seasons: the wet and the dry.

As the dry season comes to an end in May or early June, the weather becomes hot and humid. Water vapor rising from the sea fills the air with moisture, and the humid air shimmers in the heat of a fiery sun.

In a normal year, the moisture collects into low-lying clouds. Day by day, the clouds grow taller and wider, piled up into mountains in the sky by southeast winds. Thunder booms in the distance. Then suddenly rain falls in a slashing burst, and a wet grayness closes upon the land. The rain moves on, and the sun's bright light returns.

Once the rains start, they may go on all summer, falling for an hour or two every day somewhere in the Everglades. Or it may rain for a few weeks in May and then stop until late summer, when the rainy season begins in earnest.

Towering white-capped clouds march in from the Gulf of Mexico and rake the land with torrents of water. Rain slashes the plants, and drums upon the earth. Lightning crackles through the clouds, and the crash of thunder follows. A hurricane may swirl out of the sea and add its deluge to the rain that has already fallen. Sometimes half the year's rainfall cascades out of the clouds in two months' time.

In December the cool dry winter starts. The towering clouds of summer are gone. The air is fresh and sweet.

At night ground fogs mist the land, then vanish in the slanting yellow rays of the morning sun.

By late March the sun stands high and the land is dry. Cracks open in muddy places. In a dried-up watercourse, there are the marks of an alligator's sharp toes and dragging belly, made as the animal moved in search of water.

The saw grass turns gold, and the green has faded nearly everywhere. The eye says autumn, but it is really spring, and soon the rains will come again and call forth the green.

All life in the Everglades is tuned to the rains and to water that lies upon the land for months at a time. This has been true for the thousands of years that there has been an Everglades. But in time gone by there was more water and it lay longer upon the land. In those days, before man changed it with canals and levees, the Everglades was a broad, slow-moving river for nine or ten months of the year, and sometimes even longer. Its water came not only from the rains that fell on it but also from the north, from Okeechobee and the Kissimmee Valley.

Okeechobee's lake bed was shaped like a giant shallow saucer. When rains fell in torrents, the lake filled, then spilled over its southern rim. The water flowed slowly into the Everglades. Sometimes hurricane winds scooped water out of the lake and sent it southward too.

The dry season brought an end to the rains and hurricanes. But by then still more water was reaching Okeechobee. It came from a chain of shallow lakes in the

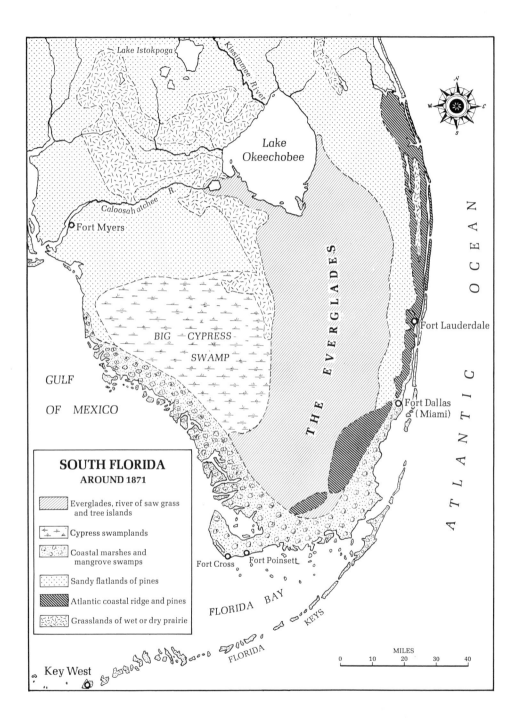

Lake Istokpoga

Kissimmee River

GULF

OF MEXICO

Lake
Okeechobee

Caloosahatchee R.

Fort Myers

BIG — CYPRESS-

SWAMP

T H E   E V E R G L A D E S

Fort Lauderdale

Fort Dallas
(Miami)

A T L A N T I C   O C E A N

**SOUTH FLORIDA**
**AROUND 1871**

Everglades, river of saw grass
and tree islands

Cypress swamplands

Coastal marshes and
mangrove swamps

Sandy flatlands of pines

Atlantic coastal ridge and pines

Grasslands of wet or dry prairie

Fort Cross   Fort Poinsett

FLORIDA BAY

KEYS

FLORIDA

Key West

MILES

0    10    20    30    40

Kissimmee Valley to the north. Filled to overflowing by heavy rains, the lakes spilled over into the Kissimmee River. The river wound slowly south, draining the rain-soaked land, spilling into marshes, and emptying eventually into Okeechobee. Again, that big lake filled to the brim and overflowed. The water flowed slowly down the Everglades.

The flow was slow because the land was flat. The southern edge of Okeechobee was only seventeen feet above sea level, and the sea lay one hundred twenty miles distant. The land fell away by about two inches to the mile. Over this flat course the water spread and crept at a rate measured in inches per day rather than the feet per second of other rivers.

Under natural conditions, at least a part of the Everglades was always covered by water. In the dry season, water covered perhaps 10 per cent of the land. Then the rains came, drenching the land, healing the cracked mud, filling the hollows, raising the water table, and starting the slow movement of water toward the sea. Later, Okeechobee overflowed and, as water from the Kissimmee reached it, went on overflowing. Water levels in the Everglades rose steadily until by late autumn some 90 per cent of the land was under water. Throughout the winter and early spring, water levels dropped and then, with the coming of the rains, began to rise again.

This annual cycle was sometimes broken by natural catastrophes. There were years when hurricanes brought bad floods, and there were also years of drought and fires.

But the many kinds of plants and animals survived. They survived flood, drought, and fire, as they survived the changing water levels of a normal year. Each kind was adapted in one or more ways to the land that was the Everglades.

The same thing is true today. That is the reason for the park, which is meant to preserve these many kinds of life. And that is also the problem, for the park does not control its own watery destiny. It lies at the southern tip of the Everglades, and it cannot control the flow of water from the north.

The true Everglades, the great river of grass, no longer exists. South of Okeechobee, land has been cleared and drained to open it up for farms, ranches, and towns. Other parts of the Everglades are now surrounded by levees to form huge swampy reservoirs. Water no longer flows freely and seasonally through what was once the Everglades. It moves instead through canals and through gates controlled by man.

Such control has put the park's life under stress and its future in danger. To be the Everglades, even a small piece of it, the park needs the right amounts of water at the right times of year, for its plants, like its animals, are adapted to the conditions that made the Everglades unique.

# Saw Grass and
# Strangler Figs

## 4

Seen from the air, Everglades National Park is a huge reach of grassy water spotted with islands and rimmed along the southern tip by dense masses of trees. It looks like the kind of jigsaw puzzle that is hard to do because it is everywhere the same. Seen closer up, the park remains vast, but it is by no means everywhere the same. An observant visitor, seeing the park from its roads and walks, soon notes that tiny differences in elevation lead to great differences in plant life.

The differences in elevation can usually be measured in inches. But in the park a few inches is enough to make one area dry land, while another is underwater for part of the year. The plant communities of the lower lying land must be ones that thrive when covered with water.

The lowest lying areas are called wet prairies, and they are covered by water for most or all of the year. A wet prairie has sparse stands of grasses and sedges. On its bottom is a thick feltlike mat, called periphyton, which is made up of algae and other microscopic plants, microscopic animals, and calcite, a mineral.

*The strangler fig is named for
the strangling embrace that its
aerial roots exert upon the host tree.*

The saw grass is also rooted beneath water for much of the year, but the areas in which it grows are slightly higher than those of the wet prairies. Saw grass is one of the oldest green plants growing today. It is extremely hardy and is well adapted to growing in shallow, moving water. Its brown flower produces a brown seed that drops from the parent plant into the water. There, instead of being carried away, it catches in the tangle of ropelike roots, where it sprouts and takes root itself.

The wet prairie and saw grass communities fill the inland fresh-water areas of the park, sharing these in places with the strangely shaped bald cypress and pond cypress, which, when they shed their leaves in winter, look like bleached skeletons of trees.

As a visitor nears the coast, he notes two changes. There is a smell of salt in the air, for the water is becoming brackish, and the landscape is dotted with scattered umbrella-shaped trees. These are mangroves. The mangroves become more and more numerous and larger and larger as the coast is neared until at last they form a dense swamp.

The mangrove swamps make up the third plant community that is rooted underwater at least part of the year. But this water is brackish or salt. Mangroves can grow in fresh water and on dry land, but they do not compete well for living space and tend to be crowded out by other trees. Unlike most trees, however, they have an ability to tolerate salt. That is why they are found clustered on swampy shores where other trees cannot survive.

There are three species of mangrove—the red, the black, and the white. But although they all bear the same name, they are only distant relatives; each belongs to a different family. Sometimes all three are found growing together, in company with buttonwood trees and other salt-resistant plants. But they may also grow in fairly distinct belts, with the red mangrove at the coastline and the other two farther inland.

The white mangrove has no outstanding feature. The black, however, can be immediately recognized by its many pneumatophores, or breathing tubes, which grow upward from the roots. They look like stalks of asparagus sticking up out of the mud or water. Both the black and the white mangrove take in salt and excrete it through their leaves. The bottom sides of their leaves are often heavily coated with salt crystals.

The red mangrove is the one visitors remember for its roots. Much of its root system is exposed, and these long prop roots arch out, like the legs of a crab, around the trunk of the tree. The red mangrove seems not to take salt in and is well adapted to life along the coast in other ways. For example, before its seeds drop from the parent tree, they develop into cigar-shaped seedlings with roots. The seedlings may take root where they fall, or they may float (continuing to grow and form roots) for long distances before they reach shallow waters and take root. The seedlings' ability to survive in the sea explains why red mangroves are found on tropical shores the world over.

The mangrove swamp, saw grass, and wet prairie communities occupy the lowest lying areas of the park. The pine forests occupy the highest ground, as they do in all of south Florida.

*These orchids are epiphytes, or air plants, anchored to the tree by aerial roots that also take the plants' food from water and air.*

The highest ground is a limestone ridge that marks the eastern rim of the Everglades. At most the ridge rises a little more than twenty feet above sea level, but that is to the north. In the park its greatest height is seven feet above sea level.

The ridge is, for the most part, bare limestone, and the pines rise from this rocky forest floor, appearing to be somehow rooted in solid rock. A closer look shows that they are actually growing out of holes in the rock that contain pockets of soil. The soil was formed by the decay of needles, leaves, branches, and other organic matter. The holes, which are known as solution holes, or sinks, may have formed by the same process — the soft limestone may have been leached away by acids produced during the decay of organic matter. Solution holes of various sizes are common throughout the Everglades.

As mangroves are resistant to salt, so the pines are resistant to fire. This is why they hold the highest, driest land, along with the saw palmettos, which are low palms. Such land is the most likely to be swept by fire during the dry season. The tall trunk and high branches of a pine tree, together with its thick bark, make the tree fire-resistant. So does the fact that it is deeply rooted in a solution hole. If the pine had shallow roots clinging to the surface of the limestone, they would be destroyed by fire and the tree would be killed. With their deep roots, the pines survive the fires that are ever a danger, as do the saw palmettos, which also have deep roots and thick bark. What burns during a fire is the understory of the pine forest—the seedlings of hardwood trees. The result is that fire plays a part in maintaining the pine forests. Fire does little harm to the pines, but it kills the hardwood saplings that would otherwise grow into tall trees, shade the pines, and crowd them out. As it is, the hardwoods grow chiefly on the tree islands called hammocks.

Tree islands are places where the land is raised a foot or two by outcroppings of limestone, the remains of ancient beaches, ridges of marl, or the shell mounds built long ago by Indians. In this flat land, even the slight ridge formed at the edges of a bulldozer trail (when a fire line is made) can become a tree island. There are two main kinds.

The smaller, lower lying islands are called heads: bay-heads if the dominant plants are bay and holly, and willow heads if the dominant trees are willow. The heads are sometimes flooded for months at a time. They support trees and shrubs that can withstand flooding and marsh plants that can withstand shade.

The islands called hammocks are slightly higher, usually larger, and they are seldom flooded. The trees that grow on them are tropical hardwoods, such as mahogany and gumbo-limbo. Hammocks, which are dome-shaped, are found in expanses of saw grass, in the pinelands, and in mangrove swamps. Their trees may be rooted in solution holes or may have shallow, widespread root systems.

The hammocks are home to many kinds of plant. Among the most interesting are the epiphytes, or air plants, which grow as aerial gardens along the limbs and trunks of trees. An epiphyte is a plant that grows upon another plant, using the latter only as support. Unlike a parasite, it obtains no nourishment from the living tissue of its host but takes what it needs from rainwater, debris, and the air.

Epiphytes are adapted to warm, humid areas, where vegetation is dense and the competition for sunlight is keen. A young plant sprouting on the forest floor has a poor chance for survival unless it can somehow break through the canopy overhead. The epiphytes "solve" this problem by growing higher up, along the branches and trunks of trees. Among the epiphytes are ferns, orchids, trees, mosses, lichens, and algae.

In the United States the great
white heron nests only in southern
Florida and the Keys. This big bird
stands four feet tall and has a wingspread
of seven feet. Its legs and bill are yellow.

A tree called the strangler fig offers a dramatic example of how an epiphyte may win its place in the sun. The seeds of a strangler fig are embedded in a sticky material within the fruit, which is a favored food of birds and mammals. When birds, for example, feed on the fruits, some seeds stick to their beaks or feet and are carried to some other tree. There the seeds of the strangler fig sprout on the branches.

The stem of the seedling puts out leaves and pushes upward toward the light. It develops a crown of its own, above that of the host. At the same time, it develops long slender aerial roots that grow down and around the host until they reach the ground. Here true roots take hold and the growth of the strangler fig quickens. The aerial roots increase in size, slowly encircling the trunk of the host in a strangling embrace that cuts off the flow of food. Meanwhile, the strangler's leaf canopy is shutting off sunlight from the crown of the host tree. Branch by branch, the supporting host dies.

While the fig is throttling its host, its roots go on growing until they cover the trunk of the host tree. By the time the host dies, the strangler is strong enough to stand on its own. As the host later decays and falls apart, the cavity it leaves is filled by the stem of the fig — the aerial roots have become a trunk.

Orchids are among the most numerous epiphytes. Unlike the orchids of more northern states, which have root systems that are anchored in soil, these are anchored to the branches and crotches of trees by aerial roots. The same roots take the plants' nourishment from water and air.

Like many other epiphytes, the orchids are adapted for conservation of moisture, which helps them survive dry seasons and droughts. Some kinds have few leaves and these leaves are small—the orchids are essentially all root. The few small leaves are tough and leathery, an adaptation that reduces the amount of water lost through transpiration. Other kinds of orchid have thickened stems called pseudobulbs (false bulbs), which store water.

Still another adaptation is found among epiphytes that are members of the pineapple family. The leaves of these plants overlap at the base but are open and spreading above. They form a series of cups, in which water is caught and stored. A large plant may have a reservoir of several pints of water, which may become a world of its own, inhabited by insects, small lizards, and frogs.

The many kinds of epiphytic fern are usually found in shady, moist places. But one, the resurrection fern, has an adaptation that enables it to extend its range and climb onto sunlit branches. When conditions become very dry or windy, the fern reacts in a way that conserves moisture. Its leaves curl up, exposing a brown underside. When there is rain or a heavy dew, the fern uncurls and "awakens" into green freshness.

Within the park, small differences determine the pattern of vegetation. They are differences in the height of the land, the amount of water, the freshness or saltiness of the water, the extent to which fire is a danger.

Red mangrove prop roots play a role in building new land in shallow bays and lagoons. Material carried in by the tides is trapped behind the roots and may eventually build up into dry land, which is colonized by other plants, while the mangroves reach out into saltier regions. The roots also protect land against storms.

The same factors maintain a balance among the kinds of plants. Hardwoods would crowd out the pines, except that they are checked by fire, to which the pines are resistant. Other trees would crowd out the mangroves, except that they are checked by salt, to which the mangroves are resistant. The saw grass holds areas that are too wet for hardwood hammocks and too dry for wet prairies.

Underlying all these small differences is the yearly cycle of wet season and dry season, of fresh water flooding the park for months at a time, then giving way to a cool dry time of mild drought. That is why any long-term or permanent change in the cycle has a far-reaching effect on the variety of plants that can live in the park and on the balance among them.

Such a change also affects the park's animal life in a number of ways. The animals, too, are attuned to the yearly cycle of wet and dry. And they are tied to the plant life. Very few of the park's larger animals feed directly on plants. But every one is dependent on plants. Green plants are the starting point of every food chain, and this is as true of the tiny algae in algal mats as it is of the big red mangroves that drop their leaves in the tidal estuaries.

# "Big Fish Eat Little Fish"

5

Among living things, only green plants can make their own food. They make their food out of simple chemical compounds that they take from air, soil, and water. All green plants, whether they grow on land or in water, produce food by this process.

All animals depend, directly or indirectly, on plant life for food. Some animals feed on plants. Some eat animals that eat plants — or animals that eat animals that eat animals that eat plants. But in every case, green plants are the basic source of energy.

The path traveled by food material as it passes from green plants to various animals is known as a food chain. Green plants form the base of every food chain. In the levels above, the animals usually grow larger and larger (big fish eat little fish), with the largest of all at the head of the chain.

Some food chains, especially on land, are very short. A deer, for example, feeds directly on green plants. This

*This big bull alligator has just snatched a good meal*
*out of a pond. An alligator does not chew its food,*
*but crushes the prey and swallows it. If the catch is too*
*large to be swallowed whole, the alligator tears it to pieces,*
*tosses the pieces in the air, then catches and swallows them.*

food chain consists simply of the green plants and the deer, unless the area has large meat-eating animals, such as panthers, that prey on deer. Then the chain has three parts.

In a slightly longer food chain, certain green plants are eaten by aphids and other small insects, which are eaten by spiders and beetles, which are eaten by small birds, which are eaten by hawks and perhaps bobcats.

In a wet prairie, the periphyton, or algal mat, is eaten by very small fishes, such as sailfin molly, flagfish, and sheepshead minnow. These small fishes may be eaten by slightly larger fishes, and all may serve as food for birds such as bitterns, blue herons, and wood storks.

In a salt-water region, ocean grasses are fed on by tiny shrimp and other small crustaceans. The crustaceans are eaten by various small fishes, which are eaten by bigger fishes. Finally, a great white heron or some other fish-eating bird (or a human fisherman) catches and eats the big fishes.

Food chains tend to be much more complicated than these examples. Most have many links and few chains are fully known. This is particularly true of aquatic food chains, whether they occur in fresh water or in salt. These are usually the longest food chains, and they are the hardest to study. To trace them, biologists must capture large numbers of many kinds of fish and other aquatic animals and then identify their stomach contents. Most of these are tiny creatures, the least-known links in food chains.

Even at the top, where animals are largest and easiest to observe and study, food chains contain surprises. The great white heron, for example, is known as an eater of shrimp and fishes; but a park naturalist photographed one as it stalked, speared, and swallowed a cotton rat, something no one had suspected the bird ate. The same naturalist came upon a purple gallinule, known as an eater of insects and snails, with egg on its face; it had just found and eaten a cattle egret egg.

Food chains are also complicated because they interlock with one another. The same plant or tiny shrimp or fish may be part of a number of different food chains. So may an insect, a mouse, or a frog. A diagram of several interlocked food chains looks like a web, and that is why a group of such chains is called a food web.

So far there have been very few detailed studies of food webs. But one was made in Everglades National Park by two graduate students at the University of Miami. They wanted to learn what part red mangroves played in the food web of the North River estuary.

An estuary is a region where fresh water from the land reaches the sea and mixes with the salt water. Like coastal marshes, estuaries teem with life, both microscopic and large. The North River food web proved to have more than eighty species of animal in it. Learning what each species ate involved analyzing the stomach contents of more than seven thousand specimens. From these analyses it was possible to trace the food pathways that began with the leaves of red mangroves.

The North River estuary is part of the mangrove area that rims the southern coast of Florida. It is a quiet region, where the silence is most likely to be broken by the fluttering of bird wings, the snap of a closing oyster shell, the splash of a fish that has jumped for a low-flying insect, or the rustle of leaves stirred by the wind.

The yearly leaf fall is heavy, about three tons to the acre. Of this only about 5 per cent is consumed by land animals. The rest becomes the basic source of energy in an aquatic food web.

When dead leaves fall into the water, they are colonized by bacteria and fungi. The leaves serve both as a place to live and as a source of food. As bacteria and fungi take in leaf material, the leaves begin to break down — that is, decay starts. As this process goes on, the bacteria and fungi are themselves grazed, or eaten, by protozoans, which are one-celled animals. Together, the leaf particles (which are called detritus), the bacteria, the fungi, and the protozoans form a unit that is high in food value for some slightly larger animal. There is some food value in the leaf particle, and there is much more in the bacteria, fungi, and protozoans. If a tiny crab or other minute animal eats such a unit, it receives a meal that is rich in vitamins and protein.

A tiny animal can digest the bacteria, fungi, and protozoans, but it cannot digest the cell walls of the leaf. It excretes these, returning them to the water, where they are again colonized. In time, the whole unit may again be eaten by some tiny animal.

Most of the tiny animals that feed on mangrove detritus are invertebrates—animals without backbones. Among them are crabs, shrimp, worms, and insect larvae. Among the small fishes that also feed on mangrove detritus are mosquitofish, killifish, sailfish molly, crested goby, and striped mullet. Many obtain 80 to 90 per cent of their food from mangrove detritus. (Most of the rest consists of algae.)

*The roseate spoonbill feeds by swinging its bill from side to side and screening tiny organisms out of the water and mud.*

The detritus feeders are in turn food for a number of bigger invertebrates and fishes. The blue crab feeds on them. So do sardines, anchovies, eels, sunfish, various species of killifish and gobies, and still others. The detritus feeders are also food for young tarpon, snook, gray snapper, red drum, spotted sea trout, crevalle jack, and catfish, all of which grow up into the big fishes that are at or near the head of a food chain.

Besides the big fishes, the top level of the mangrove food web includes a variety of other fish eaters. Among them are the alligator, the wood stork, the white ibis, the bald eagle, the osprey, and various herons, egrets, and vultures. It also includes human beings. Many of the biggest fishes are gamefish that sportsmen catch and eat. Much more important, commercial fishermen take millions and millions of pounds of human food from the mangrove food web each year. Shrimp, spotted sea trout, and blue crabs are three of the main catches that end up on our tables.

As the North River study shows, living things are closely linked in food chains and food webs, and all animal life is somehow tied to plant life. Because of the mangrove leaves, the estuaries are rich in food and that is one reason why they teem with life. A second reason is that large quantities of fresh water flow into them for part of the year. Without that flow, the shallow waters would, because of evaporation, be too salty for nearly all aquatic animals. With the flow, the waters are brackish and become a suitable nursery for young creatures such as pink shrimp. As a result, the life cycle of the pink shrimp is as closely tuned to the wet and dry seasons as is the breeding pattern of wading birds, such as the wood stork, that frequent inland marshes.

On this huge skeleton of a mangrove destroyed in a hurricane, four wood storks roost against the background of a storm-darkened sky. The two small white birds are snowy egrets, and the black bird is a turkey vulture.

# Wood Storks
and Pink Shrimp

6

The wood stork is a rare bird and the only North American stork. It lives in Florida and breeds only in the peninsular part of the state, where the two biggest nesting colonies are in Everglades National Park and neighboring Big Cypress Swamp.

A large white bird, with black feathers on its wings and tail, the wood stork stands about four feet tall on its long legs. It finds its food by wading through shallow water, scratching the mud to force its prey to the surface. Its chief food is the small fishes that inhabit the fresh-to-brackish waters of inland swamps and marshes.

Wood storks are big eaters. During the breeding season, which lasts sixty to sixty-five days, a family of two adults and two young may eat some four hundred pounds of fish. A colony of several thousand wood storks and their young requires two million pounds or more of fish during the breeding season. They take this food from waters within a twenty-mile radius of the nesting colony.

The wood stork is a grope feeder. That is, it finds its food by feel, submerging its bill in water and grabbing food that touches the sensitive nerve endings in the bill. Adult wood storks eat food as they find it. The young are fed by regurgitation: their meal is deposited on the floor of the nest by both parents.

Because they are big eaters, wood storks need a huge supply of fish. Because they are grope feeders, they need a dense concentration of fish—many fish in a small area. They must be able to feed themselves and their young and to do this without spending large amounts of energy hunting for food. A normal year in south Florida provides exactly what they need in the way of food.

The start of the wet season seems to trigger spawning among the small fishes that live in the marshes. These are chiefly mosquitofish, mollies, sheepshead minnows, and marsh killifish. As the wet season continues, surface water covers huge shallow areas of marshland, creating the best possible habitat for these small fishes and their young. They spread wherever there is water, and so do the wood storks, which fly all over Florida to feed during the wet season.

In early winter the dry season begins, and the surface water decreases. The summer's crop of small fishes is forced toward the deeper creeks and ponds. Here they are concentrated in small areas. And the start of the dry season is the time when wood storks return to their nesting grounds and lay their eggs. At the height of the dry season, the small fishes are densely concentrated. There may be four to five thousand of them to a cubic yard of water. And that is just the time when the young wood storks have hatched and are feeding hungrily on the meals their parents bring them.

Biologists think that the availability of food triggers breeding among wood storks. (The amount of daylight regulates breeding among many other species of bird.) They note, for example, that 1961 was a year of extreme drought in Florida. That winter no storks nested anywhere in the state. The reason seems to be that few fish were produced that dry summer and few were available as food when the time came for wood storks to breed. Also, there were two winters when unusually heavy rains fell. The rains increased the habitat available for small fishes, and the fishes spread out. Once they had left the ponds and creeks, they were no longer densely concentrated. The wood storks deserted their nesting colonies and returned only when water levels dropped.

For successful breeding, the wood stork depends on normal wet and dry seasons. The wet season allows for the rapid multiplication of little fishes that creates a large supply of food. The dry season concentrates the food supply. If there is too little food or if it is spread out, the wood storks do not breed. If they do not breed, they do not reproduce. Biologists suspect that food supply may regulate breeding in other wading birds too, but no studies have been made of them yet.

Studies have been made, however, of the part that the seasonal flow of fresh water plays in the life cycle of the pink shrimp. In a different way, it is as vital to the shrimp as it is to the wood stork.

Adult pink shrimp live and mate in the deep waters near Florida's Dry Tortugas Islands in the Gulf of Mexico. Spawning also takes place there, as female shrimp cast free in the water millions upon millions of fertilized eggs. Within about half a day, the eggs hatch into tiny larvae. During the first two to three weeks of life, while the young shrimp are passing through their larval stages, they are also traveling toward the mangrove estuaries. They spend about half a year there, feeding and growing to adult size. Then they reverse their route and head out to sea once more, where they live, mate, and spawn in the deep waters of Dry Tortugas.

For young shrimp the estuaries are a nursery: a safe and protected place to feed and grow. Shrimp are a major food for a very long list of fishes and other marine animals. But the danger of being eaten is much less in the estuaries than in the ocean. The ocean abounds with shrimp-eating predators — red drum, snappers, grunts, groupers. But for much of the year these fishes cannot go into the estuaries because the water is not salty enough for them; it is made brackish by the fresh water that is flowing into the sea.

The adult fishes of the estuaries are ones that can tolerate low salt content in the water: anchovies, mullet, and young menhaden are three. These also happen to be fishes that do not, generally speaking, eat shrimp. The estuaries do hold some shrimp eaters, but even so they

White-tailed, or Virginia, deer inhabit
the Everglades, ranging through marshes, saw
grass swamps, and pine woods. Here a doe and her
young fawn have come out to browse in early morning.

are much safer for young shrimp than the open sea. If the shrimp can spend their juvenile months in this nursery, they have a better chance of surviving and of making their way back to the waters off Dry Tortugas.

The estuaries also offer a rich supply of food. And there is a very interesting factor of timing, having to do with the tides and the flow of fresh water.

Mangrove leaves drop from the trees into the mud around the roots and trunks. Since the daily tides in the estuaries are not very strong, the leaf material tends to accumulate where it falls. The spring equinox, however, creates abnormally high tides. Water floods back over the marshes, tearing loose the leaf material and carrying it along. The outgoing tide carries some of this leaf material into the estuaries. The rest is trapped in the marshes, but not for long. Spring is also the time when the wet season starts. The flow of fresh water begins to carry the leaf material out of the marshes into the estuaries. And just at this time, when there is a rich supply of food for them in the estuaries, the young pink shrimp arrive.

The autumn equinox creates more high tides, and mangrove leaves are again torn loose and carried back into the marshes. Then, as the wet season ends, violent northeasterly winds begin to blow. They blow water and leaf material out of the marshes, providing food for the young of other species that use the estuaries as a nursery. And they push the pink shrimp on their way—out of the estuaries and into the ocean. The shrimp are by then adults and ready to make their run for the spawning ground.

The flow of fresh water and the mangrove food web together create an ideal place for young pink shrimp to feed and grow. The shrimp in turn play a major part in many food chains. They are also a natural resource. Commercial fishermen harvest more than twenty million pounds of pink shrimp off Dry Tortugas every year. The shrimp are worth millions of dollars to the fishermen and millions more to those who handle and process them on their way to the consumer.

The life of the park's estuaries and of its inland marshes depends on the quantity and pattern of fresh-water flow. If there is not enough fresh water or if it comes at the wrong time of year, life cycles and food chains can be destroyed. They can also be destroyed by changes in the quality of water, that is, by pollution. In the case of the estuaries and Florida Bay, pollutants can arrive in either fresh water from the land or salt water from the sea.

There are many kinds of pollutants today, each holding its own special threat. Those of greatest concern to park biologists are the ones that get into food chains. These are passed on from one animal consumer to the next, reaching their greatest concentration in the heads of the food chain. In these animals, especially birds, they are most likely to affect reproduction. That is why park biologists are studying certain animals, such as the osprey, that are the heads of food chains. They serve as indicators of what is happening in the chains of which they are part.

# Ospreys
# As Indicators

## 7

The osprey, or fish hawk, is a big eagle-like bird, with dark brown feathers on top of its body and white ones underneath. With a wingspan of six feet, it is a strong and soaring flier that haunts the skies over shallow coastal waters. There the osprey finds its food.

Its chief food is fish. When hunting, an osprey hovers fifty to a hundred feet above the water. Once it has sighted a fish, it dives feet first, catching the prey with its sharp, curved talons within a foot or two of the water's surface. Then the big bird flies off to the tree that is its favorite feeding perch. It goes day after day to this same tree, which can be easily identified as an osprey perch by the great piles of fish remains on the ground.

During most of the year, males and females do their own hunting, but at breeding time the females remain in the nest, shading the down-covered young, and the males do all the hunting. A male usually eats the head of a fish himself, before taking the catch back to the nest. He gives

*Although these ospreys
were too young to fly, they
defended their nest bravely with
flapping wings and baleful looks
when being banded and photographed.*

the fish to the female, who feeds the young. When the young are bigger and their baby down has been replaced by feathers, the female osprey may go out and hunt for herself.

Ospreys always live near coastal waters. The park has a colony of about fifty-five pairs in the Florida Bay area, where the birds have built their big saucer-shaped nests of sticks in tall trees. They fish in the shallow waters of broad grass beds and they take any kind of live fish that is easily caught — catfish, mullet, jacks, ladyfish, and others.

Because an osprey eats a wide variety of fish, it is the head of several food chains. The bottom-feeding catfish, for example, is part of one chain, while the fish-eating jack is part of another. The osprey's eating habits make the bird of particular interest to biologists who are concerned with the food chains of Florida Bay.

Generally speaking, if anything happens to break or disturb a food chain, the first victims are likely to be the animals at the head of the chain. The change will show itself in their rate of reproduction: they will produce fewer and fewer young. Therefore, a quick way of finding out about the health of a system is to look at the heads of food chains. If they are doing well and reproducing normally, then the system is healthy. If they are not reproducing normally, then something is wrong. The osprey's well-being serves as an indicator of the health of the whole Florida Bay system.

To judge how well the ospreys are doing, however, a

biologist must have something to measure against. He needs to know what is normal — the normal population level of the colony and the normal reproduction rate. The only way to learn this is to study a colony over a period of years, and that is what park biologists have been doing.

The most basic step is to mark the birds when they are four to eight weeks old, using aluminum leg bands and colored jesses — in this case small plastic bands about two inches long, with a tab that sticks out from a bird's leg. Each year's young birds are given a different color jesse so that they can be easily identified, even from a distance.

Once a marking program has been under way for several years, biologists can begin to understand the population of a colony: the age classes in it and how the colony operates. At the same time, they are gathering information about food habits and seasonal movements. They learn what the normal reproduction rates are. They learn how many young must be produced from each active nest if the population is to remain stable or to grow. An early finding of the park study was that young ospreys have a high natural death rate. Half the birds hatched each winter do not survive until the following year. Those that do survive seem to learn a great deal in their first year, for after that the natural death rate drops to 20 per cent a year.

Given such information, biologists can then ask and answer various questions. One aim of the park study is to find out what factors in the environment affect repro-duction rates. Do weather conditions have an effect? Is breeding affected by the quantity of fresh water that flows into the bay? By the time and pattern of flow? And what about the chemicals that man has added to the environment? Are they affecting the ospreys?

These chemicals are of great concern to biologists the world over. Those who work with birds are particularly worried about DDT and a somewhat similar liquid chemical known as PCB (from its full name, polychlorinated biphenyl). Both can cause reproductive failure in birds (and perhaps in other animals as well).

DDT is a pesticide, a poison used for killing insects and other pests. It belongs to the class of chemicals called chlorinated hydrocarbons. One of the problems with these particular chemicals is that they persist in the environment. Scientists know of no bacteria or fungi that break down hydrocarbons and cause them to decay. Once they are added to the environment, they do not disappear. They stay, and they are carried by wind and water to all parts of the world.

Like other chlorinated hydrocarbons, DDT does not dissolve in water. Attached to particles of sediment, DDT becomes suspended in droplets of water and travels wherever the water does. For instance, if a field has been sprayed with DDT, water draining off that field carries DDT with it. Waters meet, mix, and eventually find their way to the sea. With them may go DDT that was sprayed on land hundreds of miles inland.

DDT goes into the air when water evaporates or when the wind picks up a particle of dust that carries the pesticide. DDT that rose into the air when the dew evaporated from a treated field can be carried around the world in a few weeks. The wind gives wings to DDT.

Chlorinated hydrocarbons build up in the living things that consume them. Although they are not soluble in water, they are soluble in fat, and all living things contain certain fatty compounds called lipids. When an organism absorbs DDT, or takes it in with food or water, the DDT dissolves in the organism's fat. Once dissolved, it remains in the fat. It never passes out of the organism. This means that if an organism keeps taking in DDT, the chemical keeps building up. And once DDT enters a food chain, it is passed along from one consumer to the next.

One-celled marine plankton, for example, may keep taking in DDT, which builds up in them. Any small creatures that eat the plankton also take in the accumulated DDT. The same thing happens when the small creatures are eaten by little fishes and when the little fishes are eaten by bigger fishes. That is how DDT is passed through the food chain in ever larger amounts and becomes magnified. Animals at the top of a food chain may take in huge doses of DDT, even though the water where they hunt contains only small amounts.

Chlorinated hydrocarbons are nerve poisons. They can kill any organism that has nerves, provided the dose is large enough. This fact has long been known; it is what

*A baby-sitting bald eagle parent keeps an eye on its young, which are scanning the skies for signs of supper. Presumably this is the male parent since the female does most of the food fetching. Young eagles lack the white head feathers that account for the name bald (which in this sense means "having white on the head") eagle.*

makes DDT effective against insect pests. But something else was not known until a few years ago: a less than fatal dose can cause changes in the body's chemistry. In the case of birds, one result is that eggshells become thinner. For reasons not wholly understood, a bird that has been eating DDT-laden food produces eggs with abnormally thin shells. The shells may be so thin that they

break under the weight of the bird that laid them. If this happens, no eggs can be incubated and no young birds hatched.

Scientists in various parts of the world have come upon scenes of massive nesting failure among peregrine falcons, eagles, ospreys, pelicans, cormorants, herons, egrets, and petrels. Chemical analysis of the broken shells has shown high concentrations of DDE, a chemical compound that forms in the body from DDT.

Recently, however, PCB has also come under suspicion. PCB is a colorless, odorless liquid that has been widely used in industry for nearly one hundred years. More syrupy than molasses, PCB is used as a thickener in plastics, paints, pesticides, and chemicals for office copying equipment. It also has an extraordinary ability to stand up under heat. For this reason, it is used as an insulating fluid and as a means of transferring heat from one mechanism to another — coils and tubes filled with PCB conduct heat from furnaces to ovens and radiators, for example. PCB becomes a waste product as paints and plastics weather or as machinery is thrown away. PCB gets into the environment and, like DDT, it persists. Also like DDT, it becomes magnified in food chains of the sea.

Chemically, PCB is very much like DDT. In fact, they are so much alike that until a few years ago it was impossible to tell one from the other by microchemical analysis. Therefore, some of the damage blamed on DDT may have been caused by PCB or by the two together. But whatever the case, both cause reproductive failure in birds.

The widespread use of these chemicals poses a serious threat to many kinds of birds and worries many biologists, among them those working at Everglades National Park, where the greatest treasure is the rich bird life. An important part of the osprey study has been collecting eggs, measuring the thickness of shells, and having both eggs and shells analyzed. (Like most birds of prey, ospreys lay their eggs over a period of days, and they usually lay more eggs than they hatch, an adaptation that allows the number of young to vary with the amount of food available. The unhatched eggs can be taken for study without harming the colony.)

Analyses of the eggs have shown low levels of chlorinated hydrocarbons. The level of PCB is higher, but apparently not high enough to affect reproduction. The osprey colony seems to be a stable one. And the health of the ospreys indicates that the food chains of Florida Bay are still safe for other big fish-eating birds, such as spoonbills, great white herons, and eagles. How long they will be safe no one can say, for man continues to pour poisons into the environment.*

At the moment, however, park biologists have more reason to worry about the quantity of water reaching the park than about the quality. Periods of man-made drought have placed the life of the park under great stress, in spite of the many and surprising adaptations to natural drought.

---

* Even though the Environmental Protection Agency banned almost all use of DDT in the United States in 1972, other countries continue to use it, and so DDT still travels on the winds and in the waters of the world.

# Crayfish, Alligators, and Drought

## 8

Drought is no stranger to the Everglades. Long before man began to make changes in the flow of fresh water, there was drought. A normal dry season was a period of mild drought, when little rain fell and surface water dwindled. Sometimes there was severe drought because the rains failed. Yet the plant and animal communities survived.

How did they—and do they—survive? How can plants and animals that are adapted to life in a watery land survive drought? How can they live through even a normal dry season? Biologists cannot answer these questions for every species, but the answers they have found show an astonishing variety of adaptations.

Trees, for example, become dormant, or "sleeping," and shed their leaves. In this way, they use less water, and they do not give off water by transpiration through their leaves. The Everglades deer have adapted to a watery land by making a favorite food of the yellow spatterdock, a water lily. But in times of drought they turn

Top: *An alligator's jaws are lined with large, strong teeth. The cone-shaped front teeth are suited to catching prey, the blunt rear teeth to crushing it.*
Bottom: *When drought, whether natural or man-made, visits the Everglades, the land goes dry, the water table drops, and the surface breaks into a web of cracks.*

to other foods, and with their long legs to carry them, the deer are free to move about in search of food and water. If there is severe drought and food is in short supply, the wood stork does not nest. No young are produced and no young need to be fed. The adults fly away in search of food.

A mammal with long legs or a bird on wings can travel to find food and water. But there are many animals in the park that cannot move away any more than the plants can. Some of these share certain characteristics with the plants.

There are, for example, shallow-rooted aquatic plants that die during a drought because their roots do not go deep enough to reach the water table. But the seeds they produce are drought-resistant, and these survive. When water comes back to the land, the seeds sprout and take root. The same thing is true of eggs laid by various small creatures. The marsh killifish lays its eggs in shallow pools of water. When the pools dry up, the eggs are stranded in soil and exposed to air. But when the rainy season arrives and water begins to rise above the ground, the eggs hatch. Biologists have watched numerous mummichogs (another kind of killifish) crawl out from shallow water, lay their eggs, and die. When the rainy season returns, the eggs hatch, as do the eggs of mosquitoes and probably many other species.

If the water table is high, then to some extent the algal mats and the peat and marl soils stay moist in the dry season, drawing up water by capillary action. The eggs of some species survive in this slightly damp environment. So do adult animals.

Many of the aquatic animals survive by burrowing into the peat and marl. Among these are turtles, salamanders, frogs, apple snails, young alligators, and even certain fishes. In the mud they find moisture and protection against drying out. Catfish and bowfins (also called mudfish) are two of the fishes that can survive in mud. Both can change from normal gill breathing to skin and "lung" breathing, using the swim bladder as a lung.

A number of small creatures seem to survive drought by going down crayfish burrows to the water table below. The crayfish is a crustacean that looks something like a little lobster. It lives wherever it can find moisture — in the pine woods, wet prairies, brackish marshes, saw grass swamps, ditches, ponds, and rainwater pools. Wherever the crayfish lives, it makes a burrow. It may burrow through soil or sand into moisture, or it may make its burrow in the bottom of a deep slough, pond, or canal. By digging into the ground, biologists have discovered that crayfish burrows are used by many small creatures at times when surface water has dried up. Burrows have yielded live killifish, mosquitofish, pirate perch, salamanders, frogs, and water snakes. They have also yielded large numbers of tiny crustaceans that are eaten by small fishes.

In south Florida the rock beneath the soil is limestone, and it is extremely porous — full of small openings. Biologists think that crayfish burrow through to these

*The blimplike manatee is an aquatic animal that grazes marine plants in shallow bays and lagoons. Once hunted extensively for their flesh, manatees are now protected by law.*

openings and so reach the water table in times of drought. They think too that many other small aquatic animals reach the water table by this same route. If the drought continues and the water table sinks, the small animals descend with it through openings in the limestone. They return to the surface as the water table rises with the rainy season.

During the dry season of 1967, two biologists set up an experiment to test this idea. They selected a dried-up pond with numerous crayfish burrows and closed in the pond bed so that no aquatic animals could get in from the outside. When the wet season came the pond filled, and the biologists found that they had trapped adult killifish, mosquitofish, flagfish, and crayfish. The only way they could explain their catch was to suppose that all these small animals had risen with the water table through the crayfish burrows.

If this is correct, it helps to explain something that has long puzzled observers of the Everglades: the sudden reappearance of fishes when the rainy season starts. At the end of the dry season, large areas are parched. The mud has cracked open. Algal mats crunch underfoot. Then the rains come, and water again begins to cover the land. The water is full of fishes. Where do they come from?

Some are newly hatched and some have probably moved inland from the estuaries. But these sources do not account for the number of fishes that appear. It

*The feltlike algal mat that forms on the bottom of wet prairies later breaks apart, rises, and floats.*

now seems likely that the millions and millions of cray-fish burrows are a large part of the answer and that the small crustaceans create survival holes for many other small creatures.

With the start of the dry season, still other fishes become concentrated in the deep holes, ponds, sloughs, canals, and water-filled limestone quarries that seldom go completely dry. When water levels rise in the rainy season, the fishes spill out of these places and repopulate the waters of the saw grass swamps and the wet prairies.

Of all these places, far and away the most important are the alligator holes. In fact, without the alligators and their holes, many kinds of animals could not survive bad droughts or even the dry season. There are times when alligator holes are the only source of water for miles around.

An alligator hole is actually a small pond, twenty to sixty feet in diameter, and it is the place where an alligator lives for part of the year. The alligator's den is in the bank of the pond. Alligator holes are made by alligators and they are kept open by alligators.

Each adult alligator has a pond. A male is usually the only alligator in his pond, but a female shares her pond with her young. When the young are a year or two old, they go off on their own. They mature around the age of five or six and are then ready to settle into their own ponds.

Occasionally an alligator takes over a deserted pond or

the pond of a smaller alligator, but usually it makes its own. It may dig a pond in the open saw grass swamps, but more often it chooses a place where there is a natural hollow and then enlarges the hollow.

The alligator widens the hollow by gripping plants and roots between its mighty jaws and ripping them out of the ground. It slashes saw grass with its tail. To deepen the hollow, the alligator digs up the bottom with its hind feet. It drags plants and roots out of the pond and clears out the thicker muck by pushing or carrying it.

In addition to a pond, an alligator needs a den. If there is a suitable limestone cave, the alligator uses that. If there isn't, it tunnels into the bank of the pond, two or three feet beneath the surface of the water. It digs with its mouth and pushes the loose material back and out with its hind feet. The finished den, whether it is a cave or a tunnel, is normally filled with water except for a pocket of air.

The material that the alligator removes from its pond and den forms a bank around the pond. In this flat and watery land, a few inches of elevation make a great difference, and plants soon take root on the mud bank. Willows are among the first arrivals. Their seeds, which are carried by the wind, fall on the water, drift, and come to lodge on the mud banks. The seeds sprout, and willows quickly form a tangled hedge around the pond. Pond-apple seeds may float in, as may the seeds of other swamp trees, such as red bay, sweet bay, and wax myrtle. In this way, the rim of the alligator pond becomes a source of food for plant-eating insects, birds, and mammals. It also becomes a nesting place. Plants keep encroaching on the pond and would soon fill it in except that the alligator tears them out and keeps the pond open.

During the dry season or a drought, alligator ponds become survival holes for many kinds of life. Within them are concentrated algae, ferns, flowering plants, protozoans, and crustaceans. There are small fishes, such as killifish, mosquitofish, and sunfish, and big fishes, such as gar, bream, and bass. There are frogs, turtles, water snakes, and, of course, the alligator.

Birds and mammals are drawn to the alligator holes. Deer come to drink, otters to fish, raccoons to choose among the rich variety of foods. Long-legged wading birds join the other users of the pond, along with ducks, blackbirds, crows, and vultures. At times when the ponds are crowded with life, many of the inhabitants are eaten by other inhabitants. Small fishes eat crustaceans. Big fishes eat little fishes. Small young alligators eat minnows, tadpoles, tiny crabs, and water beetles and are in turn eaten by raccoons, bobcats, snapping turtles, garfish, great horned owls, and large wading birds. Wading birds eat fishes. Adult alligators prefer to eat garfish and mudfish, but they will eat almost anything they can catch — bass, bream, turtles, birds, raccoons, snakes, and water rats.

Even so, at the end of a normal dry season there are plenty of survivors when rains again fill the ponds to overflowing and life spreads out. Fishes, crustaceans, and other aquatic animals spill out of the alligator holes,

*An anhinga spreads its wings to dry. The feathers of its snakelike neck resemble fur.*

breeding and spawning and repopulating the waters.

During a severe drought, conditions worsen. The more shallow alligator holes dry up, killing inhabitants that cannot move away or survive by burrowing. Birds and mammals desert these ponds and so do the alligators, which travel miles overland to find water. Around the remaining deeper ponds, birds are in greater competition for food. Many abandon their nesting colonies and fly away.

The big ponds grow more and more shallow. Under these extremely crowded conditions, large numbers of fish begin to die. Some cannot survive being placed under stress for months on end. Also, the water becomes stagnant: its dissolved oxygen is used up by fishes and other aquatic animals, and the water becomes saturated with the carbon dioxide that they give off. Bass and sunfish are two species that cannot survive in stagnant water.

Other species are adapted to survive extreme conditions, at least for a time. Killifish survive because they live in the surface film of water and are air breathers. Catfish and tarpon can increase their oxygen intake by gulping air at the surface. The same thing is true of the primitive garfish, which has existed unchanged, side by side with the alligator, for tens of millions of years.

At the end of a severe drought, there are many fewer survivors than at the end of a dry season. But there are enough to keep the various species going, and if the drought is followed by several good rainy seasons, the populations come back.

At least, they always have in the past. Today conservationists worry about the future. Because of changes in the flow of water, the normal wet and dry seasons have changed. The wet season is shorter and the dry longer — it has become a kind of yearly, man-made drought. This has put the life of the park under stress. If natural drought occurs, if the rains fail, then the life of the park is in trouble.

The changes in the supply of water are of man's making. They are the result of the many short-sighted actions that have characterized the white man's approach to the Everglades.

# Man and the Everglades

## 9

The first human settlers of the Everglades were Indians. Much later the Indians were joined by small groups of escaped slaves and by a sprinkling of white hunters and trappers. None of these people made any real changes in the Everglades, for they were simply the most skilled of the predators. As such they were part of the life of the Everglades, and the pattern of life continued unchanged for many, many years. The shallow waters and the dense stands of sharp-toothed saw grass discouraged exploration by outsiders.

It was the middle 1800s before any number of white men penetrated the Everglades. In its natural state, the region seemed to them a worthless wilderness. But they noted the dark peaty soil in which the saw grass grew, and an idea took hold: perhaps the Everglades could be cleared, drained, and made into land suitable for farms and towns. Perhaps the worthless wilderness could be conquered and turned into something valuable to man.

Top: *Meandering toward the sea, fresh water cuts through mangrove forests before reaching the Gulf of Mexico.*
Bottom: *Engineers imposed the straight lines of this canal on the Everglades, forcing water out of its natural flow patterns.*

Some canals were dug in the late 1800s, but serious efforts to drain the Everglades did not begin until 1905. In the years that followed, a whole system of canals was dug to drain water into the Atlantic Ocean and the Gulf of Mexico.

With the completion of the canals, several problems became apparent. One was that the job of draining the Everglades was bigger than anyone had thought. Even 142 miles of canals were not enough.

The canals did, however, drain some of the land south of Okeechobee, and farmers moved in with sugar cane and cattle. Other problems arose. The peaty soil that had looked so rich did not seem suited to crops after all —peat lacks trace metals, and farming was a failure until agricultural experts told the farmers what to add to the soil. Then, too, exposed to sunlight, the peat began to oxidize, to vanish into thin air, a process that is still going on. Exposed to sunlight and air, the peat dried and compacted, with the result that the canals were higher than the land they were supposed to drain.

Nonetheless, the farmers persevered, and farms spread west from Palm Beach over the land south of Okeechobee. The saw grass was gone, and in its place grew sugar cane, beans, tomatoes, celery, and cabbage. Along the rim of Okeechobee new towns arose to serve the farms: Belle Glade, Bean City, Clewiston, Moore Haven.

Okeechobee itself seemed to have been tamed. There were dikes and levees along its southern rim to hold back the water, to keep it from overflowing into its natural

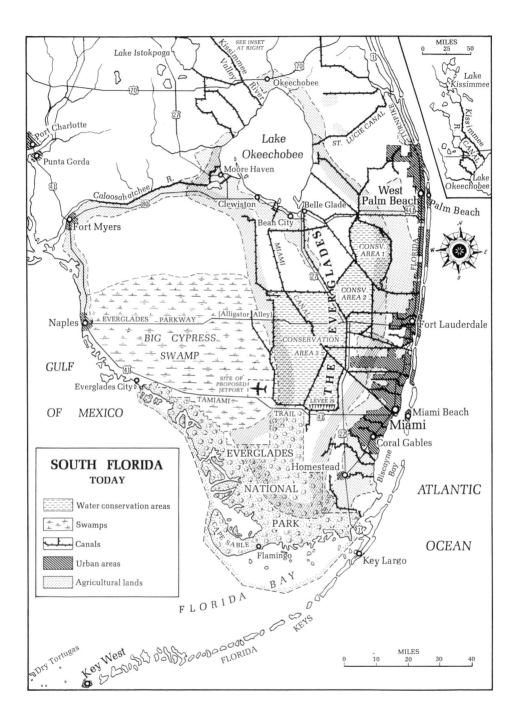

MILES
0  25  50

*Lake Istokpoga*

SEE INSET
AT RIGHT

70

*Kissimmee Valley*

70

Okeechobee

70

*Kissimmee River*

Lake
Kissimmee

*Kissimmee R.*

CANAL

Lake
Okeechobee

Port Charlotte

27

Punta Gorda

41

*Caloosahatchee R.*

80

Moore Haven

*Lake
Okeechobee*

ST. LUCIE CANAL

West
Palm Beach

Palm Beach

Fort Myers

Clewiston

Belle Glade

44

Bean City

CONSV.
AREA 1

27

CONSV.
AREA 2

Naples

EVERGLADES   PARKWAY

(Alligator Alley)

BIG   CYPRESS

SWAMP

CONSERVATION

AREA 3

Fort Lauderdale

GULF

41

OF   MEXICO

Everglades City

SITE OF
PROPOSED
JETPORT

TAMIAMI

TRAIL

LEVEE 29

41

27

Miami Beach

**Miami**

Coral Gables

EVERGLADES

Homestead

NATIONAL

PARK

CAPE
SABLE

Flamingo

*Biscayne
Bay*

ATLANTIC

OCEAN

Key Largo

**SOUTH  FLORIDA**
TODAY

Water conservation areas

Swamps

Canals

Urban areas

Agricultural lands

*FLORIDA   BAY*

Dry Tortugas

Key West

FLORIDA   KEYS

FLORIDA

MILES
0   10   20   30   40

course. To the west, the Caloosahatchee River had been dredged and deepened to carry off Okeechobee's waters to the Gulf of Mexico. To the east there was the St. Lucie Canal, draining the big lake's waters into the Atlantic.

As it turned out, however, Okeechobee was far from tamed. In 1926 a hurricane howled out of the Caribbean, tore the tiles off roofs in Miami, and swept through the Everglades. Its rain, falling in walls of water, raised the level of the lake. Then the winds hurled the water out of Okeechobee and over the southwest rim. In Moore Haven more than three hundred persons drowned. In the farmlands people had to be rescued from their homes with boats.

In 1928 it happened again. A hurricane turned inland from Palm Beach and, like a giant hand, scooped the water out of Okeechobee. This time two thousand people died. The survivors demanded action. They wanted Okeechobee held in check.

Together the state and federal governments decided on a plan to control the lake.

A massive dike, or levee, was built around the southern rim to contain the lake's waters. Meanwhile, dredges deepened and straightened channels in the Caloosahatchee and the St. Lucie to carry off larger amounts of water and so to lower the level of the lake.

By the time the work was finished, the level of the lake had dropped five feet. Several other changes had also taken place, and they were far less welcome. The water table in surrounding areas had dropped seven feet. Plants

*The limpkin is a long-legged marsh dweller that feeds chiefly on one kind of snail, the apple snail. Its limping, jerky walk earned it the name limpkin. It is also known as the crying bird, because of the loud, wailing cries it makes at night.*

withered and died as fields dried up and the soil hardened and cracked open. With a lowered water table, fresh water no longer held back the salt water. Along the coast, salt water crept inland and filled the limestone wells. With the Caloosahatchee open, salt water from the Gulf moved inland with each rising tide. Fruit groves died, and farmers had to turn to irrigation.

The effects were felt miles away to the south. The river of saw grass shrank, for the flow of water through it was much reduced. Here, too, the water table fell. Along the coast, salt crept inland, filling the limestone wells and reservoirs.

The early 1940s brought drought and with the drought came fire. There were times when the night sky glowed orange. There were weeks of smoke-gray skies, weeks when the Tamiami Trail, the highway linking Tampa and Miami, was closed because the smoke was so dense that drivers could not see where they were going. The fires raging across the flat dry land were too numerous to fight. When they had burned what was above ground, they smoldered in the peat, for peat is organic matter and can burn when dry. The end came only when the rains at last returned.

Two years later, hurricanes again turned inland, swirling across south Florida, flooding the land, and leaving behind a sea of wreckage.

Droughts, invasions of salt water, hurricanes and floods — the Everglades was not yet conquered and tamed. Therefore in 1949 the federal government joined the state

The cottonmouth is a large, thick-bodied poisonous snake that lives in swampy areas. It eats fish, frogs, rodents, and other snakes and is in turn eaten by alligators.

in setting up the Central and Southern Florida Flood Control Project. The design of the project and its construction were to be handled by the United States Army Corps of Engineers. The running of the project was to be handled by the Flood Control District. Since that time the Corps of Engineers has been digging and building in south and central Florida.

North of Okeechobee, the Kissimmee River has been channelized. The slow, meandering river no longer exists. Today water from Lake Kissimmee shoots down the straightened river, arriving at Lake Okeechobee only minutes after it left Lake Kissimmee.

This young Florida everglades kite has just returned to its favorite perch after diving to capture an apple snail in its talons. A moment after this picture was taken, the kite grasped the shell in one claw, and using its beak, separated snail from shell, dropped the shell, and devoured the snail.

In recent years, the Florida everglades kite has become a rare and endangered species. The chief reason is destruction of habitat. Many of the once vast freshwater marshes of Florida have been drained and developed. Others have been put into water conservation areas. These changes have affected the places where kites live and nest. They have also affected the apple snail, the only food that the Florida everglades kite is known to eat.

The apple snail is a freshwater snail that lives in many parts of Florida. But if marshes are drained, then the snails can no longer live in them. If there is natural or man-made drought in other places, the snails survive by burying themselves in mud, but then they are no longer available as food for the kites. If water is drawn down rapidly in the conservation areas, this affects snail reproduction. The snail eggs are laid in clusters on the stems of aquatic plants. If there is no water when the eggs hatch, the young snails cannot survive, and this affects the future supply of snails.

The Florida everglades kite can survive only if it has the natural water levels that supply it with the living place and food that it requires. Without these it will soon vanish from North America.

South of Okeechobee the land is crisscrossed with drainage canals. For about twenty-five miles immediately south of the lake, the Everglades has become farmland.

East and south of the farmland are three huge open reaches of saw grass swamp. They look like the original Everglades, but they are different because water no longer flows naturally through them. These are water-conservation areas. Each is surrounded by dikes to hold water on the land. Water reaches them through canals from Okeechobee. It moves out of them through still other canals when gates are opened.

The water-conservation areas were designed for a twofold purpose. They were meant to keep Okeechobee at a safe, nonflooding level, to protect towns and farm-lands by drawing off water from the lake. In addition, they were meant to increase the water supply for Flor-ida's east coast cities.

The coastal cities from Palm Beach south draw their water from wells that tap the Biscayne aquifer, which is a natural underground water reservoir. The Biscayne aqui-fer is composed of water-bearing limestone that lies beneath much of south Florida and that holds the re-gion's chief water supply. Water pumped from the aquifer is replaced by water that seeps down through the soil.

In earlier times the aquifer was recharged by the water of the Everglades, by water that lay on the land for nine or ten months of the year, creeping toward the sea and also seeping through the limestone. But as the northern Everglades was drained, less water flowed south and water lay on the land for a shorter period of time. Less water reached the aquifer, and this happened at a time when south Florida's population was booming, when industry was growing, and when ever larger amounts of water were being pumped from the aquifer. With less water reaching the aquifer and more being taken from it, its level of water dropped sharply. As a result, sea water flowed inland into the aquifer. City wells had to be shut down. Groves of orange and grapefruit trees died when they were irrigated with this salty water.

The water-conservation areas were intended to ease this problem. In them the runoff of fresh water is slowed, and the water is held over the aquifer for months at a time.

The decision to create the water-conservation areas marked a change in thinking about south Florida. The original idea was to clear and drain the Everglades, and the men who tackled that job never looked beyond it. Their aim was to turn a worthless swamp into productive farmland. They did create the farmland, but then it turned out that the swamp was not worthless after all — it happened to be the east coast's source of fresh water. For that reason, part of the Everglades had to be kept as swamp. But it could not be a natural swamp because there was no longer any way for water to flow naturally south from Okeechobee without flooding towns and farms. The swamp areas were diked, and water was sent into them at times when it seemed desirable to lower the level of the lake.

Yet again the planners had failed to look ahead, to see what else might happen if they diked the saw grass swamps and controlled the movement of water. They failed to foresee what might happen to the one small remaining piece of the real Everglades and to the park in which it lay, the park where all life was tuned to a yearly flow of water toward the sea.

# A Question
# of Life or Death

## 10

The Everglades, the river of grass, once covered some twenty-eight hundred square miles of south Florida. Of this, 44 per cent has been drained for farming or set aside for development. Another 49 per cent has been put into water-conservation areas.

The remaining 7 per cent lies within Everglades National Park, which was established in 1947. Here plants and animals were to live under natural conditions. Here there was to be a piece of wilderness unique in North America. Soon, however, it became clear that there was a problem and that the problem put the very life of the park in question. The problem was water.

The park had been carved out of the southern tip of Florida. It lay at the far end of the river that had once crept toward the sea. Like that of the vanishing Everglades to the north, life in the park depended on a seasonal flow of water. It depended on receiving a certain amount of water at certain times of year. The rains still

Top: *With the completion of the new Tamiami Trail
in 1963, water no longer flowed naturally into
Everglades National Park from the conservation
areas to the north. Huge flood gates can—and
do—shut off the flow, even in times of drought.*
Bottom: *Real estate speculators destroyed great
areas of the Everglades by draining wetlands, even
when the proposed community never came into being.*

fell in season, but water no longer flowed south as it once had.

By 1947 there had been forty years of digging and draining and diking in the Everglades. The flow of water had been much changed, but some still crept toward the sea through its natural course. The change had taken its toll in life, but the surviving plants and animals were adapted to the new conditions.

Within a year or two of the park's creation, there were hurricanes and floods. The Central and Southern Florida Flood Control District came into being. Its purpose, as the name states, was to prevent flooding, to control the waters of the Everglades and protect farmlands and towns. Its plans called for pumping water in and out of the conservation areas as required to prevent floods. The plans also called for releasing some water into the park.

People concerned with the park were worried. They knew that the park needed water. They knew it required flooding. They knew that it was essentially a water park. Yet they did not know how much water the park needed or how the flow should be timed, for the park was new and no studies had been made.

Long-term studies were started. They showed that a gigantic amount of water had been flowing through the park. In a ten-year period the average flow into the park through the Shark River Slough was about 250,000 acre-feet a year. (An acre-foot is the amount of water that would cover an acre to a depth of one foot.) The flow varied with the seasons. The lowest flows occurred in May and averaged 14 million gallons a day. The highest occurred in October, when they averaged 660 million gallons a day.

Another study showed the huge amounts of water lost through evaporation and transpiration. In an area of 75 square miles, the loss was 432 acre-feet, or 141 million gallons, a day.

As various studies made clear, rainfall alone was not enough to preserve Everglades as a park of life. A vast flow of water from the north was also needed.

While these studies were being made, the Army Engineers were at work. In 1962 they completed Levee 29 along the Tamiami Trail, the northern boundary of the park. Previously water had flowed freely into the park through culverts under the highway. Levee 29 shut off the flow. Built into the levee were four big structures, each with six gates that could be opened or closed with the flick of a switch. When they were closed, water was held in the conservation areas to the north. The only water then flowing into the park was that which came from Big Cypress Swamp.

The future of the park, its life or death, hinged on the gates at the Tamiami Trail. How much water would the park receive? The answer was not long in coming. When there was water to get rid of, the gates were opened. When there wasn't, the gates were closed.

Drought settled in, and the gates were closed. During the entire year of 1963 the park received no water from the north. On one side of Levee 29 was Conservation Area Three, holding water to recharge the Biscayne aquifer and for irrigation. On the other side of Levee 29 was the park. Here channels ran dry, plants withered, and small animals attempted to flee to Conservation Area Three. Deep in the park, water tables sank lower and lower. Alligator holes dried up. Wading birds failed to nest. Fish died by the thousands. Fish-eating birds, mammals, and reptiles also died. In the course of three to four years, the park lost half its alligators, and the otters were almost wiped out.

In April 1965, at the height of the drought, the park received 140 acre-feet of water. At this same time, the Flood Control District decided to lower the level of Lake Okeechobee in advance of the rainy season. Its waters were run off directly into the sea. In all, some 280,000 acre-feet of water were dumped in the sea — enough to supply the park for a whole year. Flood control in the north, drought in the south, and no way to move the water from Okeechobee to the park: that was the flaw in the flood control plan.

The situation was so serious that in the next few years several changes were made in the plan. Canals connecting Okeechobee with the conservation areas were made bigger, so that a larger amount of water could flow more rapidly south. In places the water was speeded over the flat land by pumps. A new canal was planned to run down the east side of the park, carrying water directly from Okeechobee. And finally, an agreement was signed, guaranteeing the park 315,000 acre-feet of water in all except dry years, when it must "share in adversity" with other users.

The agreement was a big step forward. It acknowledged the park's need for water and its right to water. But it was far from ideal. It said nothing about how or when the park was to receive its water, although the right timing is vital to the plants and animals of the park. Nor did the agreement say anything about quality, and quality was of concern because of an idea the Flood Control District was considering as a way of conserving water.

South Florida receives generous rainfall, and it has plenty of water. But the supply is a seasonal one, and conservation is necessary to make sure that there is water available all year round.

One way of conserving water is to store it. Both Okeechobee and the conservation areas are storage basins, but they are broad and shallow and lose huge amounts of water through evaporation. Another way of conserving water is to recycle and reuse it.

The Flood Control District was considering backpumping water so that it could be used again. Water flowing down the east coast canals was to be stopped before it reached the sea, and pumped back into Okeechobee.

The problem, as scientists saw it, was that the canals drain some of the most productive farmlands in the United States: one thousand square miles of crops that are heavily fertilized and that are heavily sprayed or dusted with pesticides. Water from such land is laden with pesticides and inorganic fertilizers. Backpumping it could have drastic effects on Lake Okeechobee, the conservation areas, and the park. The pesticides would enter the food chains. The nitrates and phosphates of the fertilizers could trigger algal blooms.

An algal bloom is a sudden and huge increase in the number of tiny green plants called algae that live in a body of water. Scientists think that blooms occur when water is overenriched, when there is a large increase in nutrients, such as nitrates and phosphates. Blooms can take place naturally. When birds roost and feed around an alligator hole, for example, their droppings fertilize, or enrich, the water, About a month later an algal bloom may occur. Blooms may also take place when water has been enriched by fertilizers that have washed off the land.

In ponds and streams that are shallow enough for light to reach the bottom, there are algae at every level. If a bloom occurs, algae may fill the whole body of water and block it. Fish can no longer live in such water. A stream's flow is much reduced. Eventually soil may slump in from the banks and block it still further. Plants and animals that lived in and near the pond or stream can no longer do so.

In deeper ponds and in lakes, algae live in the upper level of water, where light penetrates, and that is where the bloom takes place. It triggers a huge increase in the number of bacteria by providing much more oxygen and food.

The bittern, which is one of the herons, has streaked
and speckled brown feathers that serve to camouflage
the bird among the reeds and grasses of its marshy home.

Since algae are green plants, they give off oxygen by day. During a bloom there is an increased supply of oxygen within and near the mass of algae. There is also an increase in the number of dead algae raining toward the bottom, and the dead algae are food for decay bacteria.

With more food and oxygen available, the bacteria population suddenly grows greatly. It uses up nearly all the oxygen in the water. Fish can no longer live in the water. Nor can any other living thing that requires oxygen — bottom-dwelling snails, tiny crabs and shrimp, and the bacteria themselves. Among other results the base of many food chains is destroyed, and larger forms of life die or move away.

In fact, any change in nutrients can set off a watery chain reaction, even if it does not cause an algal bloom. In a marsh, for instance, food chains start with the algal mat that grows on the bottom. The mat consists of green algae, blue-green algae, diatoms, desamids, microscopic animals, and other tiny living things. They exist in certain proportions. A change in nutrients will be an advantage to some species, and they will increase. It will be a disadvantage to others, and they will decrease. And so the proportions change. Among the tiny animals that feed on the algal mat there will also be a change, for some will find more food available and some will find less — and this kind of change will pass through all the food chains that start with the algal mat.

Even without backpumping, there is reason to worry

that Lake Okeechobee is being overenriched by water flowing into it from the Kissimmee Canal, which drains a region where there is much cattle ranching and dairy farming. When the Kissimmee River still meandered south through big marshes, the plants of the marshes acted as scrubbers. There was time for them to take nutrients out of the water. When the water reached Okeechobee, it was relatively pure. But this is no longer the case. Today water and nutrients shoot straight into Okeechobee.

What happens in the Kissimmee Valley affects Lake Okeechobee. What happens in Okeechobee affects the farmlands, the conservation areas, the east coast cities, and the park. No part of the environment exists as an isolated unit.

There is no simple solution to the water problems of south Florida. Short-sighted actions of the past continue to haunt both the park and the cities of the east coast. New problems loom. There is talk of drilling for oil in the drainage area of Lake Okeechobee and in Big Cypress. Yet oil cannot be handled without accidents of some kind, and oil spills could pollute the water and destroy the plant and animal life of the park. There is the problem of use and development of privately owned land. Some lies within the boundaries of Everglades National Park. Nearly all of Big Cypress is privately owned, in some cases by large real estate companies. Other problems will arise.

A growing population requires more farmland to feed

An American, or common, egret preens itself while
perched on a pond cypress. This egret is the kind
most often found in the park. It stands about three
feet tall and has a yellow bill and black feet and legs.

it and more industries to serve it. Such growth has put increasing strain on all natural resources, including national parks.

Growth has been costly to the wildlife of the Everglades. In the 1930s, something like one and a half million wading birds were nesting in the Everglades. Ten years later their population was down to three hundred thousand, and by the middle 1950s to fifty thousand. The drainage and drought of the 1960s cut deeply into the remaining colonies.

When the park was established in 1947, it contained more than one hundred thousand wood storks. Twenty-five years later there were fewer than three thousand, and the population was still dropping. Somehow the wood storks cannot find the right combination of water and food for successful nesting. They have become an endangered species.

So has the alligator. Once there were millions of alligators in the southeastern United States. Today the alligator has disappeared from many areas, while in others its numbers almost reached the vanishing point. The park itself now contains only 2 to 10 per cent of its original alligator population. The chief reason is the number that have been killed, legally or illegally, for their hides. Today many of the remaining alligators are protected by law, but the killing goes on. Even the park is invaded by poachers.

Still, some progress has been made. Under the protection of the park, egrets are flourishing, although early in this century they were on the verge of being wiped out by plume hunters. Roseate spoonbills were once close to vanishing, but today they are increasing in number. The great white heron is no longer a scarce bird.

The most hopeful progress, however, is of a different kind. It is a progress in human understanding.

It is a growing realization that the environment must be looked at as a whole and a willingness to foresee the consequences that action taken in one place may have somewhere else.

It is a growing awareness that living things are bound together in webs of life and that we are part of those webs.

It is a sudden sense that time is growing short and that we must decide what kind of world we want before it is too late to turn back. Once the alligator, the wood stork, or any other species is gone, it is gone forever. So is a wilderness that renews human spirit and makes people feel part of the earth.

The life or death of Everglades National Park still hangs in balance, for the park has many problems. Our willingness to face and solve the problems will tell much about the kind of future we ourselves shall have.

Nearly two hundred years ago naturalist William Bartram described the scene at a Florida river in this fashion: "The alligators were in such incredible numbers, and so close together from shore to shore, that it would have been easy to have walked across on their heads, had the animals been harmless." Another observer wrote that when he raised his lantern at night, the glowing eyes of the alligators before him were as thick as stars.

Those days are gone, and perhaps it is just as well. Human beings have much to contribute to this planet's life, and we too have need of land and water. But we must learn to share. When we take everything to ourselves, we are the poorer for what we have lost. When we share with other forms of life, we are the richer for what we have saved.

# SELECTED BIBLIOGRAPHY

Much of the material in this book was obtained either through interviews with working scientists or from scientific reports and papers that are not generally available. In the following bibliography the sources most available to young readers and most accessible in terms of content have been marked with an asterisk (*).

## BOOKS

*Atkinson, Brooks. *This Bright Land*. New York: Doubleday/Natural History Press, 1972.

*Caulfield, Patricia. *Everglades*. San Francisco: Sierra Club, 1970.

*Craighead, Frank C. *Orchids and Other Air Plants*. Coral Gables: University of Miami Press, 1963.

Douglas, Marjory Stoneman. *The Everglades, River of Grass*. New York: Rinehart & Co., 1947.

McIlhenny, E. A. *The Alligator's Life History*. Boston: The Christopher Publishing House, 1935.

*Robertson, William B., Jr. *Everglades — The Park Story*. Coral Gables: University of Miami Press, 1959.

*Tebeau, Charlton W. *Man in the Everglades*. Coral Gables: University of Miami Press, 1968.

*Truesdell, William G. *A Guide to the Wilderness Waterway of Everglades National Park*. Coral Gables: University of Miami Press, 1969.

*Zim, Herbert S. *A Guide to Everglades National Park and the Nearby Florida Keys*. New York: Golden Press, 1960.

## ARTICLES, REPORTS, PAPERS, SPECIAL PUBLICATIONS

*Caulfield, Patricia. "Alligator." *Natural History*, November 1966.

Chabreck, Robert H. "The Movement of Alligators in Louisiana." Louisiana Wild Life and Fisheries Commission, 1970.

Cornwall, George W., Downing, Robert L., Marshall, Arthur R., Layne, James N., Loveless, Charles M. *Report of the Special Study Team on the Florida Everglades*. August 1970.

Craighead, Frank C. "The Role of the Alligator in Shaping Plant Communities and Maintaining Wildlife in the Southern Everglades." *The Florida Naturalist*, January and April 1968.

Heald, Eric J. *The Production of Organic Detritus in a South Florida Estuary.* University of Miami Sea Grant Program, 1971.

Idyll, C. P. "Shrimp Need Fresh Water Too." Paper presented at the Joint Convention of the Southeastern Fisheries Association and The Shrimp Association of the Americas, Miami Beach, June 22, 1965.

Joanen, Ted. "Nesting Ecology of Alligators in Louisiana." Louisiana Wild Life and Fisheries Commission, 1970.

Kahl, M. Philip, Jr. "Food Ecology of the Wood Stork (*Mycteria americana*) in Florida." *Ecological Monographs*, Spring 1964.

Klein, H., Schneider, W. J., McPherson, B. F., and Buchanan, T. J. *Some Hydrologic and Biologic Aspects of the Big Cypress Swamp Drainage Area, Southern Florida.* United States Department of the Interior, Geological Survey Water Resources Division, 1970.

Kolopinski, Milton C., and Higer, Aaron L. "Some Aspects of the Effects of the Quantity and Quality of Water on Biological Communities in Everglades National Park." A report prepared by the U.S. Geological Survey in cooperation with the National Park Service, Tallahassee, 1969. Unpublished.

Little, John A., Schneider, Robert F., and Carroll, Bobby J. *A Synoptic Survey of Limnological Characteristics of the Big Cypress Swamp, Florida.* United States Department of the Interior, Federal Water Quality Administration, 1970.

Odum, William E. *Pathways of Energy Flow in a South Florida Estuary.* University of Miami Sea Grant Program, 1971.

*Schneider, William J. "Water and the Everglades." *Natural History,* November 1966.

Tabb, Durbin C. *A Summary of Existing Information on the Fresh-water, Brackish-water and Marine Ecology of the Florida Everglades Region in Relation to Fresh-water Needs of Everglades National Park.* Institute of Marine Science of the University of Miami, 1963. Unpublished.

———. "Treasure Those Estuaries!" Proceedings of the Gulf and Caribbean Fisheries Institute, November 1965.

*Ward, Fred. "The Imperiled Everglades." *National Geographic,* January 1972.

United States Department of the Interior. *Environmental Impact of the Big Cypress Swamp Jetport.* Washington, D.C., September 1969.

# INDEX

(Page numbers in bold refer to illustrations.)

# INDEX

## ABOUT THE AUTHOR

Patricia Lauber has written more than forty books for young people, ranging from humorous fiction to factual books about human ecology. *Of Man and Mouse* was recently published by Viking. Miss Lauber has been editor of *Junior Scholastic*, editor-in-chief of *Science World*, and chief editor for science and mathematics for *The New Book of Knowledge*. She now lives in Connecticut.

## ABOUT THE PHOTOGRAPHER

Patricia Caulfield is a well-known nature photographer whose work appears regularly in such periodicals as *Audubon*, *National Wildlife*, and *Natural History*. In addition to her in-depth investigation of the fauna and flora of Florida, Miss Caulfield has worked extensively in many other wild areas in North and South America and the Caribbean, as well as in Europe and Asia.

| DATE DUE | BORROWER'S NAME | ROOM NUMBER |
|---|---|---|
| MAR 27 1980 | Young, S | 119 |
|  |  |  |
|  |  |  |
|  |  |  |